BIG DREAMS AND SHORT STORIES

25 MOTIVATIONAL SPORTS STORIES FOR KIDS

ROB LORTON

Big Dreams and Short Stories
25 Motivational Sports Stories for Kids

ISBN (Hardcover): 979-8-9949-4523-0

Library of Congress Control Number: 2026905770

Cover and interior design by Rob Lorton
Illustrations generated with assistance from AI tools.
Images are imaginative representations and are not intended
to depict specific individuals or imply endorsement by any
real person, organization, or institution.

Printed in the United States of America
First Hardcover Edition

For my awesome grandkids:
Aria, Lucas, Oakley and Willa

May you adopt the same love for reading
as your Grandma Diane, and the same love
for sports as your Pop Pop Rob

Table of Contents

Table of Contents

Hey Kids,

Every athlete in this book started out just like you — with a dream. Some dreams were big, some seemed impossible, and some took a long time to reach. Many of these athletes were told they were too small, too slow, too different, or that their goals were out of reach. But they kept trying, kept practicing, and kept believing in themselves.

I wrote this book because I love sports and I love stories about people who don't give up. These athletes faced challenges, doubts, and tough moments, but they pushed forward anyway — and that made all the difference.

As you read, I hope you find someone who inspires you. Someone who makes you think, "If they can do it, maybe I can too." Because you can. And I can't wait to see what you do next.

William Perry
The Refrigerator Who Won the Super Bowl

William Perry was a very large football player who weighed over 300 pounds. He was so big and hard to move that everyone called him "The Refrigerator."

The Fridge played defense, which meant his job was to tackle the other team and stop them from scoring. He wasn't supposed to carry the football. But deep down, he dreamed of running the ball like the smaller, faster players.

Then, one day in the Super Bowl, his coach had an idea. Coach Ditka designed a special play and even told the officials ahead of time. The Fridge lined up in the backfield, took the handoff, and rumbled into the end zone for a touchdown.

He became a Super Bowl champion and proved that even the biggest players can dream big.

Michael Jordan
From Setback to Stardom

Michael Jordan loved basketball, but he faced setbacks early on. When he was a sophomore in high school, he tried out for the varsity team but didn't make it. Most kids would have given up, but not Michael.

He practiced every day—shooting, dribbling, and running—until he could do things no one else could. His hard work paid off. In high school, he led his team to state championships. In college, he became a star and earned the chance to play in the NBA.

Michael didn't just rely on talent. He relied on determination, focus, and a love for the game. He won six NBA championships, earned five Most Valuable Player awards, and became one of the greatest players of all time.

Michael's story shows that practice and persistence can turn a dream into something real.

Bethany Hamilton
The Surfer Who Got Back Up

Bethany Hamilton grew up in Hawaii and loved surfing more than anything. She spent every morning in the ocean, practicing her balance and chasing waves with a fearless smile.

When Bethany was thirteen, she was attacked by a shark and lost her left arm. Most people thought she would never surf again. But Bethany wasn't ready to give up the sport she loved.

As soon as she healed, she learned how to paddle, stand, and ride waves in a brand-new way. It was hard, and she fell again and again — but she kept trying.

Bethany returned to competition and became one of the top surfers in the world. She proved that courage isn't about having everything go perfectly. It's about getting back up, no matter what life throws at you.

Lionel Messi
The Small Kid with the Giant Heart

Lionel Messi was smaller than most kids on his soccer team, and he faced a big challenge: his body grew slowly, and he needed special treatments to keep up with his peers. Many people doubted he could play professional soccer, but Messi refused to give up.

He practiced every day, dribbling, passing, and perfecting his control of the ball. His skill and determination grew stronger with each game.

Messi joined Barcelona's youth academy in Spain and quickly stood out. He became one of the world's best players, winning multiple Ballon d'Or awards, leading his team to championships, and dazzling fans with his speed, precision, and creativity on the field.

Messi's story shows that size or setbacks don't determine your future. Hard work and passion can help you rise to the top.

Simone Biles
The Gymnast Who Raised the Bar

Simone Biles was small for her age, but she had incredible strength and loved flipping, jumping, and flying through the air. When she was six, a coach saw her at a gym and knew she had something special.

Simone trained for hours every day, learning difficult moves that most gymnasts wouldn't even try. She fell, got back up, and kept pushing herself to be better. Her courage and creativity helped her invent new skills that no one had ever done before.

When Simone competed on the world stage, she amazed everyone with her power and confidence. She won Olympic and World Championship medals and became known as one of the greatest gymnasts in history.

Simone's story shows that greatness comes from believing in yourself, working hard, and daring to do things no one has ever done.

Kurt Warner
The Store Clerk Who Became a Star

Kurt Warner didn't start out as a famous football player. After college, he wasn't drafted by any NFL team, so he worked the night shift stocking shelves at a grocery store. But he never stopped dreaming about playing quarterback.

Kurt kept practicing, throwing passes whenever he could and staying ready for a chance that might never come. He played in smaller leagues, learned from every game, and refused to give up on himself.

One day, the St. Louis Rams gave him an opportunity. Kurt became their starting quarterback and shocked the world. He led his team to a Super Bowl victory and earned the title of Most Valuable Player.

Kurt's story shows that dreams don't have deadlines. With patience, hard work, and belief in yourself, amazing things can happen.

Naomi Osaka
The Champion Who Stayed True to Herself

Naomi Osaka grew up loving tennis. She practiced with her family every day, hitting ball after ball until her arms were tired. She wasn't the biggest or the strongest player, but she had incredible focus and a powerful serve.

As Naomi got older, she worked even harder. She studied her opponents, trained for hours, and learned how to stay calm during tough matches. Her determination helped her rise quickly through the tennis world.

Naomi won major championships and became one of the top players in the world. But she didn't just shine on the court — she also used her voice to stand up for others and speak out about what she believed in.

Naomi's story shows that strength comes in many forms. With courage, hard work, and confidence in who you are, you can make a difference both in sports and in life.

Jackie Robinson
The Bravest Man in Baseball

Jackie Robinson was strong, fast, and talented, but his greatest strength wasn't his muscles. It was his courage.

Jackie loved baseball, but in his time the major leagues did not allow Black players. Many people told him he would never get the chance to play at the highest level, but Jackie refused to give up.

In 1947, the Brooklyn Dodgers gave him his chance. Some fans cheered — but many did not. Jackie faced insults, unfair treatment, and pressure no other player had to carry. He stayed calm, played hard, and let his talent speak for him.

He became Rookie of the Year, an All-Star, and a champion — and opened the door for thousands of players who came after him. Jackie Robinson showed that bravery isn't just about strength. It's about standing tall, even when the world tries to push you down.

42

Chloe Kim
The Snowboarder Who Soared

Chloe Kim started snowboarding when she was just a little kid. She loved the feeling of flying down the mountain, carving through the snow, and trying new tricks. Even in freezing weather, Chloe kept practicing with a huge smile.

As she got older, Chloe trained harder than ever. She spent hours learning flips and spins that most riders wouldn't dare attempt. She fell plenty of times, but each fall made her more determined to get back up and try again.

When Chloe competed in the Olympics, she amazed the world with her fearless style and incredible skill. She won gold medals and became one of the most exciting snowboarders in history — all while staying joyful and true to herself.

Chloe's story shows that when you combine hard work with passion, you can rise higher than you ever imagined.

Shaquem Griffin
The One-Handed Linebacker

Shaquem Griffin loved football, but he had a challenge—he was born with only one hand. Most people would have given up, but not Shaquem.

He worked harder than anyone, learning how to tackle, block, and play at the highest level. His determination paid off. He earned a college scholarship, won a national championship, and proved himself against players with two hands. At his NFL tryout, he ran so fast and played so hard that coaches couldn't believe what they were seeing. He proved he could compete with anyone.

After three years in the NFL, Shaquem showed that heart can be stronger than any challenge. He didn't just play football—he played with courage, speed, and confidence.

Shaquem's story reminds everyone that challenges don't define you. Hard work, focus, and belief in yourself can turn obstacles into victories.

Megan Rapinoe
The Captain Who Led with Courage

Megan Rapinoe didn't just play soccer—she changed it.

From a young age, she worked on her left foot until it became one of the most dangerous in the world. Her crosses were precise. Her shots were fearless. When the pressure was highest, she wanted the ball.

In the 2019 World Cup, Megan scored six goals and led the United States to a championship. She was named the tournament's best player and later won the Ballon d'Or as the top women's player in the world.

But Megan's impact went beyond scoring goals. She stood up for equal pay and fairness in sports, using her voice to fight for her team and for future players.

Megan showed that greatness isn't only about talent. It's about courage, leadership, and standing for something bigger than yourself.

Tony Hawk
The Skater Who Spun His Way to History

Tony Hawk started skateboarding when he was a little kid. He practiced every day, trying new tricks and pushing himself to go higher and faster. Even when he fell, he got right back up and tried again.

As Tony grew older, he kept inventing moves no one had ever seen. Some people thought his ideas were too wild, but Tony believed in himself and kept working until the impossible became possible.

At the X Games, Tony landed the famous 900 — spinning two and a half times in the air — after trying again and again until he finally made history. The world cheered as he completed a trick no skateboarder had ever landed in competition.

Tony's story shows that creativity and persistence can take you farther than you ever imagined. When you keep pushing forward, amazing things can happen.

Serena Williams
The Champion Who Never Backed Down

Serena Williams started playing tennis when she was very young. She practiced with her sister Venus on public courts, hitting ball after ball until her arms were tired. Even as a kid, Serena played with power, focus, and a fierce love for the game.

As she grew older, Serena trained harder than ever. She faced tough opponents and moments when things didn't go her way — but she never stopped fighting. Her determination helped her rise to the top of the tennis world.

Serena won Grand Slam titles, Olympic medals, and became one of the greatest athletes of all time. She inspired millions with her strength, confidence, and ability to shine under pressure.

Serena's story shows that greatness comes from hard work, courage, and believing in yourself.

Derek Redmond
The Runner Who Finished with His Father

Derek Redmond trained for years to compete in the Olympics. He dreamed of winning a medal for his country.

But during his race, Derek felt a sharp pain in his leg. His hamstring had torn. He fell to the track, heartbroken—but he refused to quit.

Derek stood up and began limping toward the finish line. Suddenly, a man pushed through the crowd. It was Derek's father. He wrapped his arm around his son and helped him finish the race.

Derek Redmond didn't win a medal, but he won the world's respect. He showed that courage is finishing what you start, even when it hurts. People around the world never forgot that moment, because Derek showed that finishing with courage can matter more than winning.

Ila Borders
The Pitcher Who Proved She Belonged

Ila Borders loved baseball from the moment she picked up a baseball. She practiced every day, even when people said girls didn't play baseball. Ila didn't listen—she just kept throwing and dreaming.

In high school and college, she worked harder than anyone, learning to control her fastball, mix her pitches, and stay calm on the mound. Her determination paid off when she became the first woman to earn a baseball scholarship to a men's college team.

In 1997, Ila made even more history by becoming the first woman to pitch in a men's professional baseball league. She faced powerful hitters and loud crowds, but she stayed focused and proved she belonged.

Ila Borders showed that courage isn't about being the biggest or the strongest. It's about believing in yourself and stepping onto the field even when others say you can't.

Jesse Owens
The Sprinter Who Was Faster Than Fear

Jesse Owens didn't have much growing up, but he had speed. Running made him feel free.

In 1936, he traveled to the Olympics in Berlin, where many people didn't want him to succeed because of the color of his skin. But Jesse didn't run for them—he ran for himself, his family, and everyone who believed in fairness.

He won four gold medals, breaking records and rising above hate with every stride. Jesse Owens proved that talent and determination are stronger than prejudice.

After the Olympics, he visited schools and encouraged kids to chase their dreams, no matter where they started.

His story shows that greatness can shine even when the world tries to dim it.

Steph Curry
The Long Shot That Changed the Game

Steph Curry wasn't the tallest or the strongest player on his team. Many scouts doubted he could succeed in the NBA. But Steph loved basketball, and he refused to give up.

He practiced every day—shooting hundreds of shots, working on his dribbling, and perfecting his moves. His dedication paid off. In college, he became one of the top players in the country.

Drafted into the NBA, Steph quickly became known for his incredible three-point shooting. He won multiple championships, earned two Most Valuable Player awards, and helped change the way basketball is played —proving that skill and determination can beat size and strength.

Steph's story shows that success isn't about how big or strong you are. Hard work, focus, and believing in yourself can turn doubt into greatness.

Roberto Clemente
The Hall of Fame Humanitarian

Roberto Clemente was one of baseball's brightest stars, known for his powerful arm and fearless hitting. But what made him truly special was his heart.

Roberto grew up in Puerto Rico and worked hard to become a major league player. He faced challenges and unfair treatment, but he never let any of it stop him. He became a World Series champion, a league MVP, and one of the greatest outfielders of all time.

But Roberto cared even more about helping others. He spent his off-seasons delivering food, supplies, and hope to people in need. In 1972, he boarded a plane carrying aid to earthquake victims. The plane crashed, and Roberto was lost—but his legacy of kindness lives on.

Roberto Clemente showed that greatness isn't just about what you do on the field. It's about how you help others off it.

Rachael Scdoris
The Musher Who Saw Things Differently

Rachael Scdoris was born legally blind, but she loved dogs, snow, and the feeling of racing across the ice. She started mushing young, learning to guide her sled by listening, trusting her dogs, and memorizing every trail.

Many people said the Iditarod was too dangerous. The race was long, freezing, and filled with sharp turns she couldn't see. But Rachael didn't let doubt stop her. She trained for years, building strength and confidence.

When she finally entered the Iditarod, Rachael made history as the first legally blind musher to compete. Her courage inspired racers and fans all over the world.

Rachael's story shows that determination can guide you farther than sight. When you trust yourself and keep moving forward, you can reach places others never imagined.

Katherine Switzer
The Runner Who Expanded the Field

Katherine Switzer loved to run, but in her day, people believed women shouldn't run long-distance races. Some even said it was dangerous.

Katherine didn't believe that. She trained hard and signed up for the Boston Marathon using her initials so she wouldn't be turned away.

During the race, an official tried to shove her off the course. Katherine kept running. Her teammates protected her, and she finished the marathon with strength and pride.

Her courage opened doors for women everywhere. After the race, Katherine worked to make sure all girls had the chance to run, compete, and feel the joy of crossing a finish line.

Katherine Switzer proved that no one can decide your limits but you.

Jim Abbott
The Pitcher Who Found a Way

Jim Abbott was born with one hand, but he loved baseball from the start. He practiced throwing for hours, learning how to pitch with power and switch his glove in one smooth motion. What others saw as a challenge, Jim saw as a chance to work even harder.

As he grew older, Jim kept improving. He played in college, made the U.S. Olympic team, and earned a spot in the major leagues. Every time he stepped on the mound, he showed that determination mattered more than anything else.

One unforgettable day, Jim pitched a no-hitter for the New York Yankees. The crowd roared as he proved that heart and skill can rise above every doubt.

Jim Abbott's story shows that your abilities are bigger than your obstacles. With effort and belief, you can achieve something extraordinary.

25

Wilma Rudolph
From Polio to Olympic Gold

Wilma Rudolph was born early and very sick. Doctors said she might never walk. But Wilma refused to accept that.

She worked for years to strengthen her legs, practicing every day until she could walk, then run, then sprint. Her family supported her, cheering her on as she grew faster and stronger.

By high school, Wilma was one of the quickest runners in the country, training with focus and fire.

At the Olympics, she won three gold medals and became the fastest woman in the world. Her victories inspired people everywhere.

Her story shows that determination can turn the impossible into the unforgettable.

Tiger Woods
The Golfer Who Changed the Course

Tiger Woods started swinging a golf club when he was just a toddler. He practiced for hours, learning to focus, stay calm, and trust his swing. Even as a kid, Tiger showed talent and determination that amazed everyone around him.

As he grew older, Tiger trained harder than ever. Golf hadn't always welcomed players who looked like him, but he stayed confident and kept working toward his dreams.

When he won the Masters, Tiger made history on a course where he once wouldn't have been allowed to play. His victory inspired millions and opened doors for future golfers.

Tiger's story shows that greatness comes from skill, focus, and the courage to break barriers.

Wayne Gretzky
The Greatest Show on Ice

Wayne Gretzky wasn't the biggest or the fastest, but he understood hockey in a way no one else did. As a kid, he practiced for hours, skating on backyard rinks and learning how to read the game before anyone else could.

Wayne's vision and creativity helped him glide past defenders and make plays that seemed impossible. He broke records year after year, scoring and assisting at a pace the sport had never seen.

By the time he retired, Wayne held more NHL records than any player in history. His number, 99, became so iconic that the league retired it forever.

Gretzky's story shows that greatness isn't just about size or speed — it's about seeing possibilities where others see limits.

Tom Brady
The Quarterback Who Turned Doubt into Greatness

Tom Brady wasn't the strongest or the fastest when he was young. He sat on the bench, got passed over, and heard plenty of people say he wasn't good enough. But Tom kept working, practicing every day to sharpen his mind and improve his game.

In the NFL, he started as a backup again. When his chance finally came, Tom stayed calm, trusted his preparation, and led his team with confidence.

He went on to win championship after championship, becoming one of the greatest quarterbacks in history. His number, 12, turned into a symbol of discipline, focus, and never giving up.

Tom Brady's story shows that belief and hard work can take you farther than anyone expects.

You've just met athletes from different places, different times, and different sports. Some were told they were too small. Some were told they didn't belong. Some faced injuries, doubt, or unfair rules. But every one of them kept going.

They practiced, they stumbled, they tried again. They found courage in hard moments and strength in surprising places. And because they didn't give up, they discovered what they were truly capable of.

You have that same spark inside you. You don't need to be the fastest or the strongest. You just need to take the next step, try again when it's tough, and believe that your effort matters.

Greatness isn't something you're given. It's something you grow. And your story is just beginning.